21 Ways to be rich with Online Business

By : Vindimear D Heart

Introduction

There are many ways of making money online out there. With talents, interests and skills you already have, you just must know where to find them.

Opportunities are all around us. Ways for make money online really exist! It's important for you to know that some online job opportunities are scams, but there are many more legitimate, well-paid options for earning money online too. The only thing you need to do is to think creatively about which way you can adapt skills you already have for them. If you have a computer with an Internet connection (high-speed) and your skills. Follow this guide to reveal the best online jobs to follow, what you can expect from them, and some more interesting information about making money online.

Table of Contents

Forwards

Nowadays, there has never been easier to make money online!

Many websites and blogs earn money by selling their own online courses, software as well as other peoples products (affiliate programs).

Don't worry, you can find a lot more than ways I mentioned before to make money online.

You need to treat every program differently.

It can take some time for you to understand how everything works and which approach to use to make money from a website. If you don't succeed at first try and your original strategy doesn't work, try doing it differently . Don't give up immediately. From my experience, the main reason why people fail with making money online isn't because their ideas are bad or certain programs is not working well (it's a fraud), but because they give up way too soon.

There are plenty of ways to make money online.

There must be something that you are good at, so use that talent and earn some cash from it. Find out what interests you the most and focus on that one skill. It's super important to stick with your choice, work hard, and not be afraid to experiment whit strategy until you get it right and keep going.

Ok, now is the right time to be straight with you:

The best ways to make money online aren't free.

You always need to invest something; money or time - or both. Either way, you must pay, financial or through lots of effort developing a skill which you want to monetize from.

Now I ask you, are you willing to pay the price?

... to invest a whole month (or more) into a project you "thought" was going to be very good and fall hard on you in the end?

... to be mentally strong enough to push through obstacles and barriers that people can set for themselves and achieve your goals?

How far are you willing to go?

I will give you 21 good ways to earn money online, but I'd bet you and average people wouldn't do it. Trust me, I know that because most people are not able to answer the questions I asked you above.

In fact, they don't even consider and not to talk about letting experience it for themselves.

I am not trying to scare you. It's very important for you to know this before you don't want to waste your time... if you're not going to be serious about this. As for any goal that you want to achieve, you need to know that you will have to put a lot of effort into everything you pursut...if you want to make it as profitable and glamorous as other successful and wealthy people you see online.

So let me tell you: It's real. The results. The money. The lifestyle. It's possible but only if you manage to deal with the rough times in order to get to your goal.

Everybody has a talent, what's yours?

There are many ways to make money with skills and interests that you already have, just someone needs to tell where to look.

If you love writing

There are many websites which need part-time or full-time writers. Some of them pays people to write all kinds of reviews - for restaurants, shops, parks, events, tourist destinations...

If reviews just aren't your thing, you can earn some $ like a semi-professional writer. Following the progress of technology, new products are hitting the market every minute, and there is the job for technical writers who will explain how they work in plain English. You can write operating instructions, how-to manuals and FAQ for buyers. Over time, you will become a good writer and realize that this kind of freelancing can be quite profitable.

For example, you also can write multiple online courses and sell them on the internet. You put in the work initially, but every purchase raises your hourly rate. What I mean is:

Just overcome the old school way of thinking of doing a job one time and get paid once! Why wouldn't you do a job once, and get paid over and over again? That's your first step to great wealth.

If you are artistic

There are plenty of sites which can indulge your artistic side and you can make some extra money doing things you love.

If you are good in visual communicating and have designed your own business website or logo, graphic design could just be for you. In that case, you need to have your portfolio to show your work to potential clients. Have you designed a poster for some campaign or put together a brochure? Let the knowledge of your skills, create a website and upload images as samples of your work.

Besides that, you can join sites which are basically marketplaces for graphic design, make some mock-ups, labels, logos or something like that once and sell it over and over again.

If you are efficient and love to organize

You can be an administrative assistant for some company or business owner who can save money by hiring independent contacts to some easy and time eating money jobs. If you can perform tasks such as data entry, scheduling and transcription from your home, you can make some money from that skills. The only thing you have to do is to register with one (or more) agency which will assign clients to you.

If you are a shutterbug

You just love to photograph objects, people or nature? I have good news for you, there are companies which need all kind of images for brochures, blogs, websites and other projects. Grabe your camera, go out and take some pictures and upload them to some stock photo site. When some company buys them, you earn money. It's very important to do research before committing to any site because each of them works differently.

After reading the above, I'll give you some most common ways of making money online (which work for me and I don't see why it couldn't work for you too):

1) Affiliate marketing

2) Freelancing

The very important thing that you will see when you start working is that marketing nad freelancing are two quite different stories and require different skills. For example, writing for other people is one thing to, but making a profit from your own writing is another story. Either (ot both) of them is worth learning.

Working online besides making very good money and gaining the experience, will teach you new and good things about yourself. One most important lesson is that you only can make money online if you really care about solving other people's problems.

You probably think that it can be faked. Trust me, people can feel „your sincerity" via Skype or email. It must be your mission to solve other people's problems and then is ok to accept financial compensation for it. Just keep the best interest of others in mind and you will be sucessful and well rewarded.

Now you think that this is crap and don't even consider doing it. Ok, it's your choice but let me tell you, you are the loser here because you will remain deprived of such beautiful life lesson.

7 Great Ways to Make Money with Affiliate Marketing

From words I write above, everyone will get ideas about making money, but most of you are still confused about how to start. So I will explain how to find a website which suits your skills and expectations. Also, here you can find instructions on how to sign in and start making money from those sites. I will focus on helping you to set up your skills and make a profitable business from it.

1) SFI (Strong Future International)

It's not easy when you must decide from which site/affilate program to start when you are just the beginner in this kind of job over the net! Isn't it? My advice starts with SFI affilate site (www.sfimg.com) now when you want to deal with internet income. When I was starting my work online, I was looking for options and opportunities to make some money and came across this site. SFI caught my attention, mainly because this company exists since 1998. And successfully operating on the Internet and it's part of a larger corporation Carson Services Inc.

SFI gives you plenty of time to learn and to enter the world of affiliate marketing. At the beginning, it will take about an hour a day to do the assignment, but when you gain more experience it will take less time to do the same thing. So don't worry, this is completely normal when you just started doing this kind of job.

Ok, let's find out how to join and start working for SFI:

1. Follow the affilate link for joining SFI

The first thing you need to do is to find if any of your friends or acquaintances work for SFI and ask them to send you their unique affiliate link. If you don't know any person who already has it, just enter SFI in your browser and pick someone's invitation for joining SFI.

2. Enter details about you in blank fields

When you find yourself on the page for registration, you will see greeting from your sponsor (the person who invited you to join to SFI) and usually form for you to fill You have to write basic information about you. The very important thing for you to know is that your info is safe with SFI.

3. Hit the green „ Get Started Now!" button

Congratulations, you made a smart choice! You are now officially part of a great company! Good luck!

4. Watch START video

5. Master SFI basics

Many people don't know how SFI actually and say that SFI is such complicated site. That is way far from the truth. There are just 4 simple steps you have to follow learn how to do them. You can find the in SFI BASICS. My recommendation for you is to focus on this page ONLY and well remember what it says and then move on to other parts of the SFI Affiliate Center! You need to fully understand these basics in order to make serious money from your work.

6. Go to Affiliate Center

If you followed my previous instructions, you can continue with an exploration of the site. Go to **Affiliate Center** at www.sfimg.com and review the information on each of the tabs on your homepage. It's very important to because that is the only way for you to quickly learn all the tips and strategies to succeed with SFI. Doing that - reviewing these tabs each day, you'll be collecting valuable **VersaPoints**! So let's go through it one more time, just for you to remember: Learn SFI BASICS; review all the sections on your homepage; log in each day and apply what you learn. These actions are all you need to do to start building a great business with SFI!

7. Become an Executive Affiliate (EA)

Now I will explain why the collection of VersaPoints is so important. You need to collect 1,500 points or more to become an EA - Executive Affiliate. That is the first status on SFI and it's only requirement in order to get the commission. VersaPoints can be accumulated in plenty of ways after you register. Remember, I told you that you are collecting points just by reading lessons in SFI Basics. You can skip them just to collect points, but I recommend you to collect points in other ways (will explain it to you). It's quite simple, skipping lessons = not knowing how to collect 1,500 points for next month's.

Here are 3 most common ways of becoming EA:

Action Versapoints

You've probably heard that team building the essence of most affiliate programs online. It's a very important source from which you get valuable points which you need to become EA every month and get your commission. You need to do other important business-building actions as well. You can view how many points you get for each action you take by looking in your Ledger or To-Do List, designated by "A" in the Type column.

Website Sales

The second method for you to earn EA status is to reach 1,500 VP in sales from your TripleClicks (TC) Website (I will explain how TC in next section). It's very simple, make your own online store and refer customers to it. You can earn EA status with just one sale if you sell a little more valuable product!

Transfer Buying

You probably purchase products every day online. Why wouldn't you that same products from TripleClicks.com instead? You will achieve EA status just by buying in from SFI's marketplace. These everyday items could easily bring you 1,500 VP or more and earning you EA status essentially for FREE! This method is very good if you wish to become an EA immediately.

Note: You can qualify for EA status and collect required 1,500 VP from any combination of actions, sales, and purchases. For example, if you earn 500 VP via actions, sale products worth 500 VP and make a personal purchase worth 500 VP, you can collect 1,500 VP and earn you EA status for the month.

There are many more ways to accumulate 1,500 points or more, every month. Just follow the lessons as I mentioned before. It's all well explained, very short written and often in a humorous way. Read these instructions carefully and they will be extremely helpful for you!

That's all. Everything else you will, I believe, learn and find out if you are still interested in profits over the internet and if you decide to try this type of job.

2) TripleClick

Would you like the chance to make money using many different ways on one site? If your answer is YES, TripleClicks (www.tripleclicks.com) is the right site for you. This site is partner company with Carson Services Inc., it's a BBB member and offers you various different ways of earn money online. The interesting thing here is that you can be seller or buyer and earning money from both variants. Besides that, there are PriceBenders penny auctions which are very easy to understand, use and make some cash from it.

These are advantages of TripleClicks when it come to affiliate program:
• They handle all payments
• You get paid the moment the item has shipped
• They offer over 40 different methods of payment
• Ability to sell affiliate items/products worldwide

To become a TripleClick member, please follow these steps:

1) Follow the link that someone who is already member sent to you (or you find it online by yourself).
2) Enter basic info which is required from you on the page.

That is all, now you can start exploring the endless possibilities of TripleClicks.

It's right time to explain, one by one, how mentioned variants actually work:

1. PriceBenders Penny Auctions

This is next awesome way to make money using TripleClicks for same old auctions, but in a new and fun way that only PriceBenders Penny

Auctions can give you. Don't know how to penny auctions work? There is nothing to worry about, just follow this simple and basic explanation:

The way PriceBenders penny auctions works is quite simple. There are a new items like Mobile Phone, Laptop, Espresso Machine, TV, Headphones, Gift Card and any other stuff you can think of and you can bid for them. You also can bid for Bidding credits or TCredits at TripleClicks.

The price of the auction item starts out at just one penny. Every time someone bids, the site automatically adds one penny to the price. Most PriceBenders auctions usually start with 15 minutes on the timer which counts down to zero. Each time someone hit the red „bid now", button, the timer resets to the start time. So, as bids increase, the number on a timer is smaller in order to force the auction to close. The last person who bid when the timer hits zero is the auction winner and can buy the item he won for the price that is displayed on the timer.

Once again, TCredits are used to make bids, which can be purchased for $.29 each. On other penny auction sites on bid may cost you up to a $1 each so this is the much cheaper solution for those who love to play this game.

When it come to PriceBenders Auctions, there are many winning strategies. TripleClicks occasionally has auctions where the winner bids for free. That means that winning bidder gets all of his/her TCredits back. This is one of plenty ways to make some serious money! If you want to win on auction, it's important to have enough TCredits. My tactic is to invest fewer TCredits to win auction where the item is the package of 120, 200, 300, 400 or 500 TCredits. When I become seriously charged with TCredits, I participate in another auction for a very valuable product. If I win the auction, I sell the items I won for a huge profit. It often happens to me this situation: I win on the auction and buy the really expensive product like TV or Laptop for almost nothing and then sell it for its regular price.

You have to be TripleClicks member to have the opportunity to make money using PriceBenders Penny Auctions.

2. Member's Rewards Program (MRP)

TripleClicks awards his members for various things they do on the site. For example, you earn 5 Member Reward Points (MRP's) for each bid you make on the auction. There also an auction on which you get 10 MRP's (Double MRP Auction). The good the thing is that you can accumulate these points and then use them to buy items from the TripleClicks online store like iPods, Laptops, Audio Equipment and much more stuff. That's cool, isn't it?

You have to be TripleClicks member to have the opportunity to make money using Member's Rewards Program (MRP).

3. The Wave3 Program

The Wave3 Program is a special program for members to help spread the word about TripleClicks. Just by telling your friends about TripleClicksk, you can enjoy the following great benefits:

- 120 days free membership.

- Free MRP's! You get 300 MRP's for each referral.

- Right to download TripleClicks Song of the Month for free.

- Each month you get additional 5% discount on any one Deal Of The Day of your choice.

- For each TCredit spent by your referrals, you will receive a free bonus entry in the big Daily Crown drawing for that day .

To become a member of The Wave3 Program, please follow these steps:

1. Follow the link that someone who is already member sent to you (or you find it online by yourself).

2. Enter basic info which is required from you on the page.

That's all folks when we talking about TripleClicks.

3) Amazon

I am sure that you have heard many times about Amazon. It is the world's largest online retailer which began its life as a book e-tailer 1995.

Amazon Associates (The Amazon affiliate program) is a useful way to earn extra money if you already have (or planing to have) a blog or website. You can earn 4% or more on purchases made your blog or website using a special link. Your commissions depend on a type of product you advertise. Amazon will reword you with increasing your advertising fees after you refer more than 6 purchases every month.

Are you anxious to start making money on Amazon? Ok, just follow this simple steps and you will be ready to make decent income:

1. Make a Blog or Website

The most successful Amazon Affiliates are bloggers or have their own website. They write only quality contents adding links to Amazon marketplace. I advise you to start following these steps:

2. Use free opportunities

If you are just a beginner, start with using free solutions like Blogger, Wix, Weebly or WordPress. This way you don't need to invest money, only your time spent on designing of the blog or website and adding content to it. It's the best if you write about something you know and passionate about that, that is the only way to attract people to visit your blog or website, read and comment your posts.

3. Set up a website or blog

Amazon's marketplace can drive business away. Professional websites can also use the Affiliate program but, they are best used with people who do not sell similar products on their blogs or website. It's wise to have a website or blog and using it to promote different products, maybe some club or a service, and recommending quality products on your site or blog and make money from it.

4. Set up social media accounts for your website or blog

Social networks are very popular and crowded places and can be very much useful for your online business. This is a great way to stay in touch with you followers, improve search engine ranking, and increase the amount of links that you share. You can recommend quality products posting Amazon links on Facebook, Twitter, Pinterest, Instagram or LinkedIn.

5. Post quality content consistently

This is the only way to gain readers because people value interesting and good content. Become a writer of good stuff and post at least 2-3 times per week on your blog or website.

6. Gain loyalty of the readers

For start, you should avoid that readers of your blog or site don't have feeling that your goal is to make money from them but to share new experiences with some product that you bought and think that is good. So put Amazon affiliate links as recommendations, make a list of the best vendors, compare products. The most important thing here is to be frank with people who follows you and make sure that only good products find their places on your site or blog.

Note: Having fun with posting links = more likely to sell. For example, you may write a post about the best non-fiction books of the year, Hollywood blockbuster or the year's most innovative new products.

Include links to Amazon products and people will trust your choice and use the link as a reference and buy the item..

Signing Up for Amazon Associates is very simple:

1. Go to www.amazon.com. - affiliate-program. It's very important for you to read through the information thoroughly before signing up. You should understand all the term and all the information about products, how to use affiliate links and how to get paid before starting an account.

2. Hit the "Join Now for Free" button if you are ready for registration.

3. Enter your Amazon username and password. Select your official payment address from a list or type it.

4. Fill out the basic information about your site, web traffic, and online monetization. Then enter all of the sites you will use to post Amazon links.

5. Verify your identity.

When you finish with your registration, follow this instruction:

1. Start looking through products on Amazon's Associates Central.
2. Choose a few products to integrate into your blog posts. It is a good idea to use the "Bestseller" filter to find the bestselling products in any category.
3. Post the link inside your website. You can choose to post an image, an image and text or a text link, depending upon how you want it to look.
4. Use the Amazon Associates site stripe, the toolbar at the top of the page, to capture links for products you want to post.

4) eBay

Every successful affiliate marketer knows that eBay (http://www.ebay.com) is a great program for selling any products online. It's simply because eBay offers you a pretty big potential audience of 147 million members. And people who read about your product probably know that it can be found on eBay.

eBay is very similar to Amazon and way to way to market affiliate products on it are the same. The point is that you interest people who read your posts to a list on you special link with you unique code (affiliate), which will take him/her to the owners sales page and purchases the product. You job here is done. The owner will handle product delivery and reword you with your sales commission payment.

I have to tell you, setting up an auction on eBay is not that easy. I have no doubt that you will write a very good post about how marvelous your affiliate products are and certainly attract a number of people who would be interested in buying. But there is one problem, there is no legitimate way of selling it to eBay members! eBay don't allow you to have a link in your auction page which takes your readers away from the.

I will share with you two ways how you can enter the eBay market with having your affiliate products:

1. One penny auction

You create an auction and explain which are the benefits of the affiliate product you want to promote. The important thing is that you sell the information where people can buy that good product. Basically, you sell details about the product (let's say) for one penny.

When someone buys your information, you need to send him/her an email and thank him/her for purchase. Next step is to explain that he/she don't really have to send you a penny, and write down the link to the awesome product, the same one they purchase information for. Naturally, that link is with you unique code (affiliate link).

Tip: Try to be as original as you can. If your auction appears to be one of many, people wouldn't notice yours among others. Putt on your auction product description with personal and credible information, that is the good way to "convince" some of those prospective customers to go with you.

It could happen that eBay remove your one penny auctions because it doesn't bring eBay very much are removed by eBay. After all, a one penny auction doesn't bring eBay very much from the final value fee.

So, if you have bad luck and this happens to you, try system 2 below. Also, try to do the same thing (system one) on other auction sites such as Amazon or Yahoo.

2. Create a package of products for $0.99

This second strategy is a little harder and requires researching before launching eBay auction for the affiliate product. The goal here is to make a package of products which are related to your affiliate products and auction at $0.99.

Create a report (2 - 3 page) about your affiliate product in a personal manner. You should write it to sounds like it's based on your personal experience with the product. don't forget to input your affiliate link in it.

The next thing you need to do is to locate other products for your "package" by using Google search to find related free items.

Example: If you are an affiliate for an ebook which teaches people how to paint and draw portraits, It's normal that you will search on Google for something like " portrait drawing" for free. Be careful not to give away something that can compete with your affiliate ebook.

When you find wanted items, add them to your 2-3 page report and create an auction for 99 cents.

No way that eBay will object to this auction.

One thing is clear, all it really takes to be successful affiliate marketer on eBay is to putt some creativity in it.

5) Rakuten Affiliate Network (former LinkShare)

You rarely can find affiliate marketing networks which are eager to make easy and profitable long-term partnerships between advertisers and publishers. Rakuten Affiliate Network (www.marketing.rakuten.com) is website wich promise premium technology to all members - a technology platform for the search marketing management, marketing training, consultative services. Advertisers have constant help with:

- Generating new sign-ups
- Registrating
- Leads
- Applications
- Free trials

As affiliate marketer Rakuten Affiliate Network, you will receive advice that drives results. Their expert account managers are focused on your best interest and will help to achieve your marketing goals and protect your brand. Besides that, they will work with you on identifying the best potential publishers for you and designing of service level appropriate to your goals. You have access to thousands of publishers who are recruited every day worldwide and search them by product category, traffic, consumer geography...

Very important the thing is that every publisher must meet certain requirements before they can qualify for Rakuten Network membership and are monitored for compliance on a daily basis. The program provides makes sure that publishers are well trained to meet your needs thanks to coaching and incentives from sites affiliate team.

These are benefits that Rakuten Affiliate Network can offer:

- Accurate, reliable technology
- Dashboard reporting features to help you identify actionable trends and other criteria meaningful to your campaign.

- Patented tracking technology ensures report accuracy
- Easy tools to upload ad links, coupon links or product feeds
- Reliable online payment options

If I manage to convince you to try making money with this awesome network, sign up by following this steps:

Enter your contact information.

1. In the business details section, you need to select a range for Annual Online Revenue and Unique Site Visits Per Month.
2. Choose 1 Primary Service Interests (Affiliate Marketing, Display, Paid Search or Attribution) and Other Service Interests (same choice as for Primary)
3. Type questions in notes/questions section.
4. Hit red " Submit" button.

6) CJ by Conversant

Commission Junction (www.cj.com) has been on the market for years, and the company has a brilliant reputation as being one of the leading affiliate advertising networks. The network attracts many well-known advertisers that visitors of your blog will already be familiar with, making it more real that they'll click on an ad and make a purchase (and that means higher earnings for you).

A great aspect of CJ Affiliate by Conversant is that once your application is accepted, advertisers within the network might ask you to join their individual affiliate programs within their network. One day, you might just get an email inviting you to join an affiliate program through the Commission Junction network, meaning you can outflank the individual program application process and start displaying ads for that program right away!

The Commission Junction Website is very easy to navigate has a reliable payment system, and help is always available if you need it. A large number of advertisers in the network offer a variety of ad types such as banners, text link ads display ads (various size image ads), and much more stuff.

It can be difficult to be accepted into Commission Junction affiliate program because the network attracts a lot of big advertisers. You have to fill out an application, then you have to apply to each advertiser's program individually (if you're accepted). Therefore, it can happen that you might not be able to get accepted into the individual affiliate programs whose ads you want to display on your blog, even if you were accepted into the Commission Junction network.

There are no two same programs, every single one is different and it's up to you to make the choice. Because of that, it's very important to take the time to read all of the requirements and payment terms for each individual affiliate program that you join the Commission Junction network. Make sure that the payouts and requirements meet your abilities and goals.

Commission Junction affiliate advertising network is a great program for you to join. Before you apply on the Commission Junction Website, be sure that you have the order with all information and then fill out the Commission Junction application.

Getting started with affiliate marketing is remarkably easy. Make sure that your site is perfect for affiliate network ads and then you can start by following these steps::

1. Go to Commission Junction and click the Publishers tab.
2. From the Publishers next step, click on "Free Publisher Sine-up".
3. From the Publishers page, click the "Sign Up Today".
4. Select the radio button for a language you prefer, choose your country from the drop-down list, and select a currency, and then click the "Next button".
5. On page 2 of the application, scroll down to the bottom and click the "Accept" button. Select the radio buttons for the Code of Conduct, Privacy Policy, Age Certification, and Certification of Authority policies.
6. In the Site Information section, enter the name of your blog in the Web Site or Newsletter Name text box, and enter your blog URL in the Web Site URL field.
7. In the Website box for the description, enter few words about your blog, putting an accent on the aspects of your content that are most relevant to your affiliate network application.
8. Select your general topic from the Category drop-down list.
9. Just get as close as you can to the best match for your site; you can change this later if necessary.
10. Select the range of visitors you have from the Current Monthly Unique Visitors drop-down list.
11. Select the appropriate check box(es) in the Define Your Promotional Methods section.

12. Disclose whether your site gives specific incentives to its visitors; if so, describe your site's incentives in the text box.
13. Fill in the information in the Contact Information and Company Information sections, and then choose the method of payment.
14. Enter what you see under the Please Enter the Characters into the Box Below into the text box, and click the "Accept Terms" button.

After you complete and submit your application, you need to can wait 24–48 hours before your application is reviewed and either approved or rejected. Nearly all applications to affiliate networks are approved unless they suspect that your site is have something to do with illegal or unethical activities.

Basically, the first thing you have to do is to apply to join programs and post banners and text links after you've been accepted. It's very important that you don't apply to any affiliate program until you're established with a good niche site so that you can get the best possible chance of getting approved.

7) AvantLink

AvantLink (www.avantlink.com) is leading technology platform for affiliate marketers. For this site's clients it implies consistent improvement and updates to the platform, fast implementation of new tools and technology, and emphasizes on quality over quantity.

If you want to build your niche site, monetize existing one or take your affiliate marketing to the next level, AvantLink and Altrec.com will take you there. Altrec.com has the best gear and performance clothing available. Avantlink is developing a dynamic tools that are unmatched in affiliate marketing. These programs together can help you to build traffic, increase conversion and make more money online.

Here are more highlights:

- Totally FREE Sign-up
- Over 3000 products from the most famous and best selling brands like Nike, Burton, The North Face and many more.
- 10% Commission on every sale.
- Earn an extra 1% seasonal commission on all sales from October through February
- 4 months to refer a sale and earn the commission (cookie duration of 120 days)
- Feeds that have more content to boost your conversion and SEO, as well as dynamic cross links, color swatches, user reviews and more.
- Great Dynamic Tools like link builders, datafeeds, banner, coupons and more.
- Awesome Program Manager which will help in optimization of your site, answer questions and basically help you make more money.

If AvantLink is you choice for making money online, follow these steps to registrate and start working:

1. Go to AvantLink.com and select "Affiliate" tub.
2. Hit "Get started" button.
3. Sign up for Affiliate.
4. Sign up for a network you like (US, Canada or Australia.
5. Enter basic details about you and your website.
6. Carefully read terms and conditions and privacy policy.
7. Hit the blue "Sign Up for AvantLink".

7 Great Ways to Make Money by Freelancing

In this chapter, I will explain how to find freelance a website which suits your skills and expectations. Also, here you can find instructions on how to sign in and start making money from those sites. I will focus on helping you to set up your skills and make a profitable business from it.

1) Upwork

I am very excited to write about such an amazing website as www.upwork.com (used to be oDesk.com), a platform that very efficiently connects employers with freelancers. It's one of the world's largest freelance talent marketplaces which is created in order to connect businesses with great talent faster than ever.

Freelancers are earning more than $1 billion Upworking for businesses of every size, from the one-person startup to a major corporation. Everyone can be freelancer here, if he/she is seasoned executives or college students, lawyer or transcriptionist, from Boston or Bolivia. This platform offers a world of work opportunities, provided by a network of 3,100,000 individual contractors, for all skills you can think of - that can be done on a computer. Upwork offers more than 2700 skills in categories including this services:

Web Development

Software Development

Networking & Information Technology

Writing & Translation

Administrative Support

Design & Multimedia

Customer Service

Sales & Marketing

Business Services

What makes Upwork.com so special for freelancers?

Payment Structure

When you are freelancer on Upwork, you can choose two different ways in which you want to get paid for the job:

Fixed Price

You negotiate with an employer how much you want to be paid for a particular service. When you agree about the price, the employer gives you a deadline for finishing the job.

Hourly

The employer pays you per hour for the job. The platform allows your "boss" access to the Work Diary, which has screenshots from the actual work you are doing. He/she can do that via Time Tracker program which keeps the record of what you being doing and for how many hours on the particular job.

Fees

The Upwork Service Fee is 10% of the total amount charged to the client. The fee is paid automatically each time your client is charged on a contract. Your clients don't this fee when they fund for the job. I recommend you to always include this fee in total charges when you talk to clients because they will only see the total billing rate.

As it comes to month subscription and posting, they are FREE on Upwork.

Simple hiring process

When we talk about hiring process on Upwork, it's quite simple. Clients create job post with all important details about what he/she expect from freelancer to do and how much is the budget. When you go to "Find Job" tab you can see many posts for different jobs, depending on which skills you entered in your profile. Find the job that suits you and apply for it. Fill your application by entering the amount which you will be charge to the client, selecting estimated time for finishing off the job from a dropdown menu. You also need to write your cover letter and attach a file with the sample of your work if clients ask for it. Also, I really appreciate the quick hiring process. It's basically a 1-click process once you know who you want to work with.

You can see all the reviews and feedback from previous freelancers about employer

The real value is that you can see all the reviews and feedback from previous freelancers about the employer before you apply for the job. If the particular client has mostly positive feedbacks will be fair with you and you will have good communication.

Test for freelancers to make their skills better

Upwork.com offers many tests that freelancers can perform which can make their skills better. It can be a bonus for you if you have passed some hard tests with great result and your potential employer can see that and how good you really are.

More than enough times to bid for jobs per month for free

Connects are virtual tokens you need to submit in order to apply for a job. If you're invited to apply or are being rehired, you won't need to use any Connects. All other applications require anywhere from 1 to 5 Connects, depending on factors such as the size and type of job. Initially, most jobs require about 2 Connects.

There are 60 Connects at your disposal per month for free. If that isn't enough you can buy extra Connects for $1 each.

2) PeoplePerHour

PeoplePerHour (www.peopleperhour.com) was founded in 2005 with offices in London and New York. It's a marketplace whose mission is to connect freelancers and small companies worldwide in a trusted environment where they sell and buy services to each other. This network counts about 250,000 active users (180,000 freelancers and 70,000 clients). The majority of employers using PeoplePerHour services are small businesses that don't want to hire full-time professional workers. In other words, thousands of small companies use this site every day to find and hire really talented people without employing them the old fashioned way, which allows a flexible relationship between them.

PeoplePerHour offers a wide range of businesses that rely on freelance marketplaces run the from web development and design firms to accountants and lawyers.

Here is list of all categories:

Design (WebSite & App, Arts & Illustration, Logo & Identity,Business & Advertising, 3D, Animation, Books & Magazines,Label & Merchandizing,

Video, Photo & Audio (Video, Image editing, Audio, Photography, Voiceover, Music, Filmmaking)

Web Development (Custom Website, Mobile website, Other, eCommerce, WordPress, Blog, Newsletter/Email template, Social app)

Sales & Marketing (SEO, Sales/Calls, Business data, SEM/Adwords/PPC, Strategy/Research, Email marketing, Other, Press release)

Business Support (Typing/Proofreading, Other, Business services, VA/Admin support, Accounting/Tax, Data research, Excel/VBA, Presentations)

Writing & Translation (Web Content, Business & Marketing, Copywriting/Proofreading, Article, Technical writing, Creative writing, Translation, CV/Cover Letter)

Social media (Facebook marketing, Twitter marketing, Youtube marketing, Linkedin marketing, Instagram marketing, Pinterest marketing, Google+ marketing, Social bookmarking, Forum marketing)

Software Dev & Mobile (Mobile Development, Databases, Software testing, Java, Game development, C++, Visual basic, Data mining)

How to make money using your skills on PeoplePerHour

There are 5 steps you need to follow if you want to monetize from your skills as an individual freelancer on PeoplePerHour:

1. **Attract clients with a profile that's built to sell**

Your profile is the first thing that tells a potential client a lot about you. The point is to impress the Buyers that you are competent enough to offer you a job. To build you profile you need to fill your complete profile in a way that information about you, photos, and previous work experiences must be a perfect marketing mix. Make sure that your profile photo looks professional by putting clear image which show your face. So use it to tell your story, add you photo and videos and make it fun.

Note: PeoplePerHour ranks profiles based on economic activity per month which gives newbies a chance to move up.

2. Make a portfolio which will prove that what you write in your profile is true.

Let's clear one thing for good, a profile without a portfolio is a weak profile. Your portfolio is some kind of catalog of skills that you really possess . For example, if you are a web designer, you should include links to sites you designed for past clients.

But, if you are new to all this, you must be wondering how you are supposed to have a portfolio. Well, if you don't have a portfolio, make this clear in your profile. Then you need to upload samples of your previous work or link to samples. If you haven't got any samples to show, create some.

3. Search for Jobs and send a direct Proposal

On PeoplePerHour, you (as a seller) can send direct proposals to Buyers on a job that is listed. So trough yourself on searching for jobs relevant to you and start sending proposals to the ones you think you can complete easily. Every seller has a limited number of proposals that he/she can send, only 15 proposals per month for free. Be very careful about who you are sending a proposal to.

Tip: If you are just a beginner here, try to pick the easiest jobs and create great proposals to minimize the chances of rejection

4. Post Hourlies

Hourlies are short promotional packages designed by PeoplePerHour for sellers. The concept is similar to what we can see on Fiverr so you tell the client in a few words what you can deliver within a specified period of time at a stated price.

For example, if you're good at Web designing, you can post an Hourlie and it can look like this: " I can design a five-page website for $100 in one day". This gives a potential client the opportunity to purchase your hourlie on the spot. So, add samples, photos and descriptions of your previous work (to convince the Buyers with your skills), hit the post, and watch the cash coming to you! ☺

That is the best way for you to use Hourlies as a quick way to make money. so make sure you take advantage of this great opportunity.

5. Getting paid

When you earn some money and want to withdraw it, you have to do this easy steps:

1. Go to the Payment section.
2. Use the Withdraw Funds link.
3. Choose Paypal or your Bank account to transfer your money to.
4. It takes 1 working day to process your request for payment.

3) Fiverr

Simply put, the best definition for Fiverr (www.fiverr.com) is that this is a place where you can sell and buy tasks for $5. This is unique site because it's the only mobile marketplace online which offers services as a product. Fiverr Isn't about hiring the freelancers but the service they provide.

Other freelancing sites putt freelancers in position to compete against others, so they often focus on offering the cheapest price rather than quality. To avoid that, Fiverr allows individuals to offer their services as products, to become entrepreneurs and create their own brands. For that meter, it's in providers best interest to get positive reviews and opportunity to provide additional services for an added value. Besides that, if you do well and offer high-quality services, Fiverr continues to promote your gigs and increases your ability to offer new services and new prices.

When you complete your order successfully, you will be paid $4. I know, I earlier said that every gig costs $5, but Fiverr charges you $1 fee for each gig. Now you probably think that Fiverr is not really worth your time. That simply isn't completely true, you need to try a little harder to be in the position to offer good gigs to people. I am more than happy to tell you that, I know few people who are making a living online doing just selling gigs on Fiverr. In fact, I just bought a car from the money I made from Fiverr.

You can do it too if you have basic or advanced (even better) skills from these categories:

Graphics & Design (Cartoons & Caricatures, Logo Design, Illustration,Book Covers & Packaging, Photoshop Editing, Flyers & Posters, Business Cards & Stationery, Banner Ads, Social Media Design,3D & 2D Models, Web & Mobile Design, Presentations & Infographics, Invitations, T-Shirts, Vector Tracing)

Online Marketing (Web Analytics, Article & PR Submission, Blog Mentions, Domain Research, Fan Pages, Keyword Research, SEO, Bookmarking & Links, Social Marketing, Get Traffic, Video Marketing, Reviews)

Writing & Translation (Business Copywriting, Creative Writing, Translation, Transcription, Resumes & Cover Letters, Proofreading & Editing, Press Releases, Articles & Blog Posts, Research & Summaries, Legal Writing)

Video & Animation (Commercials, Editing & Post Production, Animation & 3D, Testimonials & Reviews By Actors, Puppets, Stop Motion, Intros)

Music & Audio (Mixing & Mastering, Jingles & Drops, Voice-Overs, Sound Effects, Session Musicians, Producers & Composers, Singers & Songwriters)

Programming & Tech (WordPress, Web Programming, Mobile Apps & Web, Website Builders & CMS, Convert Files, E-commerce, User Testing, QA, Databases, Desktop Applications, Data Analysis & Reports, Support & IT)

Advertising (Hold Your Sign, Flyers & Handouts, Human Billboards, Pet Models, Outdoor Advertising, Radio, Music Promotion, Banner Advertising)

Business (Business Plans, Career Advice, Market Research, Presentations, Virtual Assistant, Business Tips, Branding Services, Financial Consulting, Legal Consulting)

Lifestyle (Spiritual & Healing, Health & Fitness, Relationship Advice, Online Private Lessons, Astrology & Fortune Telling, Travel, Cooking Recipes, Diet & Weight Loss, Makeup, Styling & Beauty, Parenting Tips, Animal Care & Pets)

Gifts (Arts & Crafts, Unusual Gifts, Video Greetings, Handmade Jewellery, Greeting Cards, Postcards From..., Gifts for Geeks, Recycled Crafts)

Fun & Bizarre (Just for Fun, Your Message On..., Extremely Bizarre, Pranks, Celebrity Impersonators, Dancers, Daredevils & Stunts)

I'm pretty sure I managed to convince you to try making money on Fiverr. If I'm right, follow this simple instruction:

1. Go to fiverr.com.
2. Click on "sign up" button.
3. Enter your email address and password.
4. Wait for the confirmation of your email address.
5. Create your first Fiverr gigs and start making money online from it.

4) Freelancer

Freelancer (www.freelancer.com) is one of the largest freelancing marketplaces which mission is to connect freelancers and employers worldwide. On this site employers have at disposal freelancers of all professions to hire. It has a platform that allows you to advertise your talents and make money from them from the comfort of your home. As you can see, Freelancer is very similar to UpWork, so you don't need to be surprised by the fact that they are the largest competitors.

The strongest side and greatest advantage of that kind of sites is that they provide instant access to thousands of independent freelancers with specific skills to employers, without the need for advertising of the job, providing work space, insurance, etc. For the freelancer, they offer a constant source of work opportunities (part-time or full-time), without the spending any money or time for advertising or self-promotion.

Being part fo such great network as Freelancer, you can enjoy the ultimate opportunity called job flexibility! You can choose what you will work, when and where you want.

If you like Freelancer's lifestyle, sign up for free and try it. Registration si simple, just make this few step:

1. Go on Freelancer.com.
2. Click on "SIGN UP" in the top right corner.
3. Fill up empty boxes with your details and hit orange "Create account" button.
4. Complete your account details.
5. Select your skills and expertise.
6. Verify a payment method (Credit Card, PayPal or Skrill).
7. Confirm your email address. When you submit the registration form, Freelancer will send a message to the email address you provided at sign-up. Follow the link in the email to activate your Freelancer account.

If you're done with all from the previous instruction, the only thing left for you to do is to create your profile and you can start bidding for jobs. So take a few minutes to enter some information about you. This your opportunity to present yourself to Freelancer community as a person and professionally. It's important to fill out your profile completely. Make Be sure that you are uploaded a photo to your profile because it's much better if contractors can relate with your face, not only with a username.

The subheading is a good place to make a good first impression. It might be some kind of slogan or just a list of the top skills you can offer. The goal is that subheading make other users want to know more about you. Then they will visit your summary section to get to know you a little bit more.

This is your chance to really make your profile stand out from the others. So write about your professional mission or your work history. Highlight your skills and let people in the Freelancer.com community know why you're the best freelancer for the job.

Projects

Projects can be are posted only by registered employers. The job post should include descriptions, skill requirements and a budget range. Freelancers must use the project board to search for job posts that match their skills and interests. When they find applicable projects, freelancers place bids and provide additional information and additional work samples through a private messaging system. If employers estimate that you are the most qualified bidders, he/she will award you.

Fonding and withdraw options

Each registered Freelancer.com member has the own free online account for fund transfers. You can withdraw funds from your account via wire transfer or direct deposit to an online account (PayPal, Skrill). An optional debit card is also available that provides members with immediate access to the funds in their accounts.

You can withdraw money on a weekly basis. Minimal fees to offset processing costs may apply to certain transfers and are deducted when the transfer is initiated. Freelancer.com Fees (10% or $5.00) will also be deducted from members' accounts as applied.

Feedback and Rating

When a project is completed, if payment is made within the Freelancer.com system, the rating and feedback system for that project is activated. This allows you and your employer the opportunity to rate each other's performance on a simple 10-point scale and to leave comments. It's good that you may also post a response to your employer's comments. This ratings and comments can been seen by other members so it's very important to have good ratings and feedback (cumulative rating and ratings for individual project) to help other members to see the value of working with you.

5) Toptal

Toptal (www.toptal.com) is a global network of elite software developers. Their mission is to understand client's needs and connect them with pre-screened developers who join their teams for a full-time, part-time, or hourly jobs.

The Toptal network has army of thousands of developers from about 100 countries. They have this specialty: Software Engineering, iOS, Ruby on Rails, LAMP, NET, Java, Python, JavaScript, C++, C#, HTML5/CSS3, PHP, Scala, Objective-C, SharePoint, Salesforce, Android, Node.js, Django, MATLAB.

If you are software developers with some of listed specialties and want to be accepted into the network, you must pass a screening process that includes tests:

- English and communication skills tests
- Timed algorithm tests
- Live coding exercises
- Test projects

Toptal is a very different working platforms from UpWork or Freelancer which typically work at much lower rates. They are more focussed on hiring top level Software developers, with a cost of a $7000 - 12000 per month for each developer if they are working full- time.

I am not so closely acquainted with TopTal but I believe that this is a whole new story, when it comes to companies for Software developing , mostly because they are who are hiring people to work at their facilities. TopTal is different and they look for remote developers that will work from home and open to contracting freelancers as well.

My best friend is a member of Toptal network for almost a 2 years and his overall experience is pretty good. He found an excellent long-term customer. Because of that and a great community of developers, he says that he can't imagine doing anything else. It's possible to have as much work as he wants, and he can stop whenever he wants. Joining Toptal was the best decision for his career and I can testify that. Based on his expirions, I can highly recommend you to join, or at least try to pass a screening process.

Signing up as developer goes trough next steps:

1. Go to toptal.com.
2. Hit green " Apply as a developer" button.
3. Then click on " Join Toptal" button on Developer portal.
4. Fill application and hit " Join Toptal" button again.
5. Pass the screening process.

6) 99designs

99designs (www.99designs.com) is leading online marketplace for graphic design. Their mission is to make quality design accessible to all people. It's a place where people can find good graphic designers for creating logos, T-shirts, websites and much more stuff. The customer start-up contests for designers with information about what they exactly what and then chooses the best work which owner will win a cash payment.

The way 99designs is functioning saves customer's time because they don't need to go through large numbers of freelancers' portfolios to be able to choose the right one for the job.

They also can work with individual designers by purchasing design templates from 99designs' Readymade logo store.

99designs has over 850,000 designers who are ready to create all the different designs someone needs. They work in many categories:

- Logo Design
- Business Card Design
- Brochures
- Mobile Apps
- Clothing and Apparel
- Book Covers
- Websites

Here what graphic designer need to do in order to make money on 99designs. The procedure is quite simple, just follow this steps:

1. Find a contest

There are about 3,000 contests open at any time. I'm pretty sure that you can find one that fits your skills.

2. Submit your design

Read the details about the job, create a design and collaborate with the client.

3. Win and make money

Try to make your best with every design create. That is the only way to win more contests and to make more money.

4. Keep it going with a good stuff

If you are good and your clients are satisfied with you work you can Continue working with him using 1-to-1 Projects. Approximately 50% of the projects resulting in additional direct jobs and that are the reason why we can say that 99designs is really a powerful tool for making money and building client – employ relationships.

So if you want to join the design community and start earning money, the only thing left to do is to sign up and become a member of 99designs. Follow this steps:

1. Register by entering your email address and password.
2. Enter unique nickname for your account.
3. Finish editing your profile (inculde your representing photo and portfolio).
4. Start searching for contests.

7) Creative Market

Join me and have a peek in what Creative Market (www.creativemarket.com) is all about and how this site is different from other marketplaces online.

Creative Market is a marketplace which allows people to sell and buy digital creative products online in a simple and beautiful way. If you are a graphic designer or some other kind of independent creatives, you can sell, themes, graphics, stock photography, brochures and other digital items for use by web designers. Since our world is always online, there are more and more work for software developers and they need help with all kinds of templates that will improve workflow.

The basic idea behind Creative Market is familiar. Their mission is to fill the blank canvas with the simple and beautiful design which are accessible to everyone.

There are five different categories of products people can buy:

Photos (Abstract, Animals, Art & Entertainment, Beauty & Fashion, Architecture, Business, Education, Food & Drink, Health, Holidays, Industry, Nature, People, Sports, Technology, Transposition)

Graphics Graphics (Icons, Illustrations, Objects, Patterns, Product Mockups, Texture, Web Elements) from $5 up to $60.

Templates (Websites, Brochures, Flyers, Resumes, Stationery, Business cards, Invitations, Magazines, cards, Presentations, Logos, Email) for less than $10.

Themes (WordPress, Tumblr, Drupal, Bootstrap, Jamie, Ghost, HTML/CSS, Magento, Open Cart) around $60.

Fonts (Serif, Sant Serif, Script, Display, Symbols, Blackletter, Slab Serif, NonWestern) from $2 to $25.

Add-Ons (Actions, Bruches, Gradients, Layer Stiles, Palletes, Shapes, Plug-ins) under $10.

Why is Creative Market Unique?

It seems that they are doing things pretty much differently comparing with other creative marketplaces.

There are few primary strategies which are really impressive for me as a seller:

70% Commission

You don't have to start at a low commission and work your ass off in order to insure your way up to something decent. Every seller keeps 70% of their sales. Trust me, this is a very good rate and something that will really emphasize this site from others.

You Decide on the Price

On other creative marketplaces like GraphicRiver, you upload the item and they automatically set the price for it. I think that that kind of sites policy isn't fair because you put a lot of hard work and dedication into your creation only to have someone else decide how much its worth. It's great that thing aren't like that on Creative Marke because you have complete control over pricing your items. Isn't that cool?

No Exclusivity Promise

The big players, such as iStock Photo or GraphicRiver, demand that your sell your stuff only trough their site or they drastically reduce your commission rate if you're not willing to sign their exclusivity agreement. If that is the case, GraphicRiver you can get only 33% of the price from your item. You will agree with me that game just isn't fair. The advantage of Creative Market compared to other is in fact that they simply don't care about that stuff. Sell your goods on other sites or be exclusive, it's your choice.

No Reviews

If you've ever worked as a freelancer before, you are familiar with the drill. You worked your ass off to create something that you can sell well and your item was rejected simply because reviewer woke up on the wrong side of the bed. I can be very frustrating. Creative Market gives you an opportunity to sell whatever you want to sell. If your stuff is no good, your ratings and reputation will sink. If your reputation is good that means that your items are great too. That is the sign that potential buyers can trust you.

That Local Feel

Creative Market is trying to distance itself from the feel of overrated larger stock sites. That is only one more impressive unique selling propositions from them. Their philosophy is to "open a shop" instead of simple uploading and selling items. The point is that they make that personal connection between seller and buyer. Creative Market wants to introduce customers to the great people behind the products. This is pretty brilliant from my perspective.

How to become a seller on Creative Market?

To become a member of Creative Market, you need to be invited. Another way is to apply through their partner page. Maybe this kind of barrier may deter some sellers, but I think that it helps with keeping the quality of the items high. It's to the mutual benefit of customers and shop owners. And let me tell you the best part: when you're accepted into the marketplace, you can upload files for sale immediately. There is no review process to wait for and you can start making money right away.

7 Great Ways to Make Money Selling Your Products

In this chapter, I will explain how to find a website where you can sell your own products. Also, here you can find instructions on how to sign in and start making money from those sites. I will focus on helping you to set up your skills and make a profitable business from it.

1) TripleClick

At the beginning of the previous chapter, I was discussing TripleClicks (www.tripleclicks.com). It was mentioned that there are several ways of making money and one of them is by selling your own products.

These are advenages of TripleClicks when it come to selling your products:

- They handle all payments
- You get paid the moment the item has shipped
- They have an army of affiliates that can sell your products for you
- They offer over 40 different methods of payment
- Ability to sell your items/products worldwide

Now is the perfect time to explain how selling your own products actually works. You have two options:

1. Garage Sale

On TripleClicks, you can organize garage sale online and sell your old items or any other things that you no longer use. Only thing you need to do is to list item, on by on, and it will cost you only US $0.29 per item and it stays up on the site until it sells with no further fees. I think that this is the only site which gives you the opportunity to list a product with up to 700 words of description and three pictures for less than 30 cents. You do that once and the only thing left for you to do is to wait for someone to buy it. Then you get paid with no other charges. Other sites are less favorable because they have much higher fees for listing your products and, if you don't sell them within a certain period of time, you have to pay again

Registration for this program is very easy, just follow this 4 steps:

1. Register as a TripleClicks Member
2. Purchase some TCredits
3. List your items

2. The ECA Program

Using of TripleClicks Ecommerce Associates program (ECA) is similar to any other online marketplace. You have the opportunity to set up your own online store within the main TripleClicks site. Things are very simple here, just list a number of products, sell them and get paid. The major difference between this program and others is that you have to pay only $40 for the license and you can sell as many items as you like. The more you show your products in a good, professional and unique way, the more goods you will sell...for less time and easier.

Major benefits that TripleClicks ECA Program offers are:

- Ability to reach millions of customers all over the world on e-commerce sites that is growing with lightning speed.
- Has 100,000 affiliates at its disposal. They will promote and sell your products in over 20,000 cities and 190 countries worldwide.
- Simply sign up.

Registration for ECA program is very easy, just follow this instruction:

1. When you get link from someone who is already a member, follow it and click on marked place – To get started, sign up here.
2. Do the same thing on the FAQ page.
3. Enter your private , public and product information
4. Read the participation agreement and chech if you agree
5. Enter your account information
6. Verify your documents (just follow the instruction on the page)
7. Comfirme your ECA application by clicking on „Continue" button
8. Repeat step 7) for your participation agreement

And that's it. Now you have to wait for your ECA to be approved. You will be notified by email.

2) Etsy

Etsy (www.etsy.com) is a marketplace which connects people around the globe who want to buy, create and sell their unique stuff. Besides sites I mentioned here before, Etsy has it's global community consisting of creative people who use Etsy to sell what they make, the customers who are looking for buy things they can't on other places, manufacturer companies who want to be partners with sellers and help them grow, and CEO , executive team and other staff who maintain and trying to make their marketplace such an inspiring place.

There are 3 categories of products you can sell on Etsy:

Handmade Goods

Vintage Items

Craft Supplies

It's free to join and sett up a shop on Etsy. You can list items for costs $0.20 USD each. When your listing is published it lasts for four months or until the item is sold. When you sell your product, Etsy will assess a 3.5% fee on the item's sale price. So make sure to carefully read their terms and then accept the fees that they will charge you before publishing a listing.

If you still not sure that you want to sell your creative items on Etsy, I will give you few more reasons:

- Buyers from nearly every country worldwide.
- 1.4M creative businesses and 20.8M Active buyers.
- Make your brand, share it with a whole army of new customers using good promotional tools.

- Communicate with experienced sellers and experts in Etsy Teams and Online Labs.
- You can be an Etsy member for free.
- Express your creativity and make money from it.

You can get your payment using your credit card, PayPal account or via check. When you sell your item, buyer pay (credit or debit card) in his local currency you will receive the funds to your bank account in your local currency. Also, you can accept payment methods such as PayPal, check or money order as an alternative to a credit card.

It's very simple to Sign up and become the seller on Etsy. I will walk you through the registration process:

1. Go to the Etsy site and click on " register for an Etsy account here".
2. Enter your basic detail and hit button for registration.
3. Then click on "Open a Shop" button at the bottom of the site.
4. Confirm your language preference and currency in which you list items. Be carefull what language you will choose because it will be your shop's default language and once is set, it can not be changed later. You will only be able to enroll in other languages after opening your shop. You can change your currency after opening your shop.
5. Set up your shop. Just follow the instruction and complete each of the steps.
6. Choose the name for you shop. Make sure that name you want for your shop isn't already used by another person.
7. Add listings. Just follow the instruction and complete each of the steps.
8. Get paid. Select the payment methods for buyers on your shop. Your options are: Direct Checkout (The main way to get paid on Etsy); Credit/debit cards (Visa, Mastercard, American Express,

Discover, Carte Bleue (France)); Etsy Gift Card; International and mobile payment methods (currently available to shops in some countries); PayPal; Check or Money Order.

9. Open your Shop. When you do all previous step, click Open Your Shop on the right side of the last section.

Congratulations! Your new shop is now open!

The web address leading to your new shop will be:

https://www.etsy/shop/yourshopname

    or

https://yourshopname.etsy.com

3) eBay

eBay (www.ebay.com) is a good way if you want to make money online by selling your own products. Then set up your store, you don't need programming experience and it can be done in minutes. It's that simple to open the store on eBay because they do all the background work for you and your visitors will use the regular eBay bidding engine. In other words, when you setup a store, eBay will create auction site for you. You can customize certain aspects of it (like title, links or more) and it's staggered on ebay.com's domain.

Now I will reveal one big secret to you, but you have to promise me that you wouldn't tell anyone about it. ☺ If you want to get traffic to your Auction Site, create another site in addition to your eBay store. then I highly suggest you to that if you want that people can find your auction website in search engines like Google, Yahoo or any other. Here's why...

Your auction page, that eBay will give you, can be promoted using the website address which will look like this:

http://stores.ebay.com/your_store_name

Ok, now you have website address but the problem is that it sits on eBay's domain and if you tried to submit it to Google, for example, it would be ignored because it is considered as a duplicate site (sub-site) within eBay. Yahoo or Google just don't add this kind of site to their directory because there's no point in adding all of eBay's stores when people can just go to the eBay's home page and search for it there.

The key to getting traffic to your unique eBay auction store, overcoming the above-mentioned problem, is to create a separate site with your own domain (yourstore.com). This is the only way to have the content that the popular search engines and directories can find. So create your site and link it to your eBay auction store and start selling your products.

Registration steps:

1. Go to ebay.com. and find a link to "Sell" at top right corner.
2. Click the "Register" button.
3. Fill out the form (just follow the sites instructions).
4. Carefully read the User Agreement and Privacy Policy.
5. Click "Submit" button if you agree with them.
6. Confirm your registration (An email will be sent to you, open it and click "Submit" button).

Now you are become an eBay member but if you want sell your own products, you need to have Seller Account. Just follow these instructions and create your Seller Account:

1. When you finish with registration for eBay account, you will automatically land on a Welcome page. Click on "Start selling" button.
2. Then on "Step 1: Get Ready To Sell"
3. Hit the "Register to sell" button.
4. Enter your User ID and Password.
5. Review the steps to get started and then press "Continue" button.
6. Review your information. Point out if you have a physical store. Mark the checkbox to verify your information is correct. If you're made a mistake, click the "Edit" button to make changes.
7. Press the "Continue" button.
8. Confirm your phone number. The Site will send you 4-digit PIN and you can choose to receive it by phone call or a text message. You will receive it within a few minutes.
9. Enter your PIN and click on "Continue" button.
10. Select the payment method (from PayPal, credit/debit, or bank account) and fill out the corresponding information.
11. Read carefully the billing agreement and hit the "Agree and continue" button.

And that's it, you're ready to start selling!

4) Evanto Market

Envato Market (www.market.envato.com) is leading marketplace created to help you get creative and make some money. It is a home for many people who like to create images, themes, project files or stuff like that. There are thousands of talented creators of all kinds, from designers to developers, who sell tones of their own digital items and assets. Envato Market has own slogan is: "You Do Creative, We'll Do the Rest". See for yourself is it really true using one of 8 sites from this list:

ThemeForest (categories: Site Templates, WordPress, CMS Themes, eCommerce, Blogging Marketing, Forums, PSD Templates, Muse Templates, TypeEngine Themes, Static Site Generators)

CodeCanyon (categories: JavaScript, PHP Scripts .NET, WordPress Plugins, CSS, HTML5, Mobile Apps, Skins, Edge, Animate Templates)

VideoHive (categories: After Effects Project Files, Apple Motion Templates, Motion Graphics, Stock Footage, Cinema 4D, Templates, Add-Ons)

AudioJungle (categories: Music Packs, Sound Effects, Source Files, Logos & Idents)

GraphicRiver (categories: Graphics Print Templates, ePublishing, Textures, Vectors, Infographics, Add-ons, Isolated Objects, Icons Presentation Templates, Fonts, Web Elements, Logo, Templates, T-Shirts, Game Assets)

PhotoDune (categories: Animals, Architecture, Business, Food, Health, Sports, People, Technology, Travel)

3Docean (categories: 3D Models, Cars, HDRI Images, CG Textures, Materials & Shaders, Base Meshes, Scripts & Plugins, 2D Concepts, 3D Print)

ActiveDen (categories: Flash, Flex, Unity 3D, JSFL Extensions)

ThemeForest

ThemeForest is the largest of the Envato Market sites. Many people say that ThemeForest is the home of web designers and developers which create HTML templates, themes for popular CMS products and much more. There you can find everything from WordPress themes to the website, email and e-Commerce templates. The price of products depends on the complexity, quality and use stuff like that and includes a Buyer Fee. ThemeForest is the biggest marketplace of its kind.

CodeCanyon

CodeCanyon is the place where you can sell and buy scripts and components for a plenty of languages and frameworks (including JavaScript, PHP, ASP.NET, and Java). The price of products depends on it the complexity, quality and use stuff like that and includes a Buyer Fee.

VideoHive

On VideoHive site, you can sell or purchase royalty-free footage and motion graphics. Besides that, there are also After Effects Project files people can buy for just a few dollars. The price of products depends on the complexity, quality and use stuff like that and includes a Buyer Fee. VideoHive you can call the home of motion graphics junkies!

AudioJungle

AudioJungle is part of Envato Market where you can sell and buy sound effects (completely Podsafe) as well as royalty-free music for just a few dollars (Buyer Fee included). The site is home for audio composers and producers.

GraphicRiver

GraphicRiver is one of the biggest marketplaces for graphic designers who are experts in creating , layered Photoshop files, Adobe add-ons, vectors, logos, icon packs, brochures and design templates for just a few dollars (Buyer Fee included). The price of products depends on the complexity, quality and use stuff like that. The best graphic designers and illustrators just love this site.

PhotoDune

In the short time the latest Envato marketplace has been online, we've seen a lot of positive signs about PhotoDune :

- The collection size is already above 400,000 and growing quickly.
- Best contributors are saying great things about PhotoDune.
- And perhaps best of all, the CEO of the company, is spending a lot of time communicating directly with microstock contributors on top forums.

This thing I just listed is proof that PhotoDune is one of the best regular microstock startups and also distinguish it from the established agencies. This is the main reason why PhotoDune brings a large existing customer base to Evanto Market.

3Docean

3Docean is the exelent place for all people who want to make passive income from their 3d work. That is the reason why they are looking for 3D/2D artists who are willing to help with setting the new standards for new marketplaces with similar products.

ActiveDen

If you want to build Flash and Unity 3D projects faster with video players, music players, games, image galleries, animations and much more stuff, do not hesitate to become the member of ActiveDen. This is the right site for you.

The primary difference which gives an advantage to Envato Market over its competition is definitely the background of the company. Envato Market has eight successfully grown marketplaces for the digital asset. That is the main reason why this site has a large number of existing members. Most of them are buyers with registered payment details. So, what are you waiting for, register as Envato Market member and you will automatically be signed up for all eight sites.

1. Go to Evanto Market website and click on "Create an Envato Account" link.
2. Enter basic details about you and click green "Create Account" button.
3. Comfirme you registration clicking on the link in email site sent to you.
4. Complete the process of creating your account.

5) E-junkie

E-junkie (http://www.e-junkie.com) is a shopping cart and digital delivery system for publishers who have their own website and want to sell their own products online. Use it to sell physical products on your site. For physical products, you can include details such as color and size options, shipping and packaging and more. Pricing starts at $5 per month and with this package you can list up to 10 products within a 50 MB space limit.

There are two categories of items:

Downloads (mp3 songs and albums, e-books, icons, fonts, software, etc.)

Physical products (CDs, books, phone cards, event tickets, posters, t-shirts, etc.)

You can sell on your blog or website, social media, other marketplaces, etc. If you use E-junkie you can copy-paste buy now buttons and shopping cart to let you sell digital and physical products. It's possible to manage your products from their admin panel while selling your products on multiple places at the same time.

E-junkie is taking care of interfacing with the payment processor you want and also do secure and automatic delivery for your digital products. They support payments from all PayPal options(Standard, Advanced, Pro), ClickBank, Google Checkout, Payflow Pro, TrialPay, Authorize.Net, and 2Checkout. There are no bandwidth limit, no transaction limit, no setup and transaction fee. If you have monthly subscription all fee are covered and you have right for full usage of E-junkie to sell online for the month.

Now I will tell why you should consider selling your own products on E-junkie:

- **Easy to use, centrally managed service.** The only things you need to know to use our service is the name and price of your products. Just copy E-junkie's "Buy Now" button codes (which you get from Seller Admin) to paste into the website. No installation and programming required!

- **Instant and secure product delivery.** After a successful payment for digital items you are selling, customers will be redirected to the instant download of your product. He/she will get the download link(s) in the "thank you" e-mail.

- **Store your files securely on our server, or remotely on your own server.** E-junkie's system will automatically issue to each of your customer the unique, secure and expirable download link to obtain an exact copy of your file after their payment is confirmed as complete.

- **Sending out free expirable download links.** It's possible to use E-junkie to send free copies of the product to your reviewers or friends. Also, you can send it just to yourself to test things.

- **PDF Stamping for E-book security.** You can identify the person who shared your file if you do happen to bump on a copy of your e-book you sold via E-junkie. So each copy of your PDF eBook file can be stamped with their name, email address, and unique transaction ID, which can discourage sharing of your property in that way.

- **Manage your inventory automatically.** E-junkie gives you the opportunity to set a date-time and the quantity limit for all products you are selling. This is a very useful feature if you want to sell physical items, limited circulation articles, event tickets, phone card codes, etc.

- **Autoresponder, updates, and newsletters.** You can send updates and newsletters to any customer group. In that way, all your customer will be automatically placed in the group of the product they have purchased and you can also manually add other people to customer groups.

- **Customization.** In E-junkie Admin > Preferences, you can add custom HTML/JavaScript/CSS for the whole "Thank You" page. Also, you can customize each product to have it's custom HTML/JavaScript/CSS shown on the "Thank-you" Page. It's possible to configure an email with a "Thank You" note, instructions and anything else you want for each product you sell.

Registration for E-junkie is simple.

My advice is to first to login using Demo User Account and see if you like the site. Just go to http://www.e-junkie.com and click on " Start FREE 1-week trial now " button in the bottom left corner of the Sellers page. Then click on "Go" button and enjoy the ride. ☺

Then try the free trial. Just go to http://www.e-junkie.com and click on " Start FREE 1-week trial now " button in the bottom left corner of the Sellers page and fill in the form for free trial registration.

If it turns out that E-junkie is the right place for you, register for the seller and start making serious money online.

6) Shutterstock

Shutterstock (www.shutterstock.com) is a global marketplace for artists and creators to sell royalty-free images, footage, vectors and illustrations which are. Still dominates that part of the market, regardless the fact that it's the pioneer of the microstock sites. Shutterstock still sells more photos than any other similar website and earning this is the main reason why still stands among top micro stickers' earning agencies.

If you have your artists side and love to creator images, vectors and/or illustrations, Shutterstock is the right place for you. This site counts customers from 150+ countries which have paid over $300 million to their sellers/contributors. This is great opportunity for you to make money just by doing things you love. Besides photos, you can sell footage, video clips and pieces of music as well.

So If you have a camera with a decent resolution and love to take pics, you definitely must consider making some images for microstock sites and make some cash.

We want to see the world through your eyes.

Steps to register on Shutterstock:

1. Go to Shutterstock.com and click on " Become a Contributor " link you can find in top right corner.
2. You will lend on Shutterstock Contributor page. Hit " Sign up now" button.
3. Create an Account by entering basic details about you. Review Terms of Service and click on red "Continue " button on the bottom of the page.
4. Verify your e-mail address.

Congratulations, you just made your first step to become a Shutterstock contributor! Now you must show if your work meets customers' criteria. You need to:

1. Choose what you want to upload (Images, Vectors, Illustrations or Videos). Read carefully requirements and press " Upload " button.
2. Upload your ID – They accept a passport as document and then upload 10 Images you think that YOUR ORIGINAL best work and click on " Continue" button.
3. Wait for Shutterstock to review your request.
4. You will get an email from them when/if your work meets their criteria.
5. Upload your creations and start making money.

Tip: Shutterstock search function in a way that new photos have better chances to be sold. Most recent and well-sold pics maintain high search positions. That way they continue with good selling. Because of that, images of modest quality quickly fall down in the search results and they are not easy to find by potential buyers.

7) Fotolia

Fotolia (www.fotolia.com) is third largest image bank (just behind Shutterstock and iStockphoto) with over 42 million images, vectors, illustrations and video clips and more than 5 million customers for affordable, royalty-free images, graphics and videos wich will give their brochures, websites, reports and slides much better look.

Just like any other Microstock site, Fotolia has its own community of graphic designers, artists, and agencies which are bringing thousands of new and unique images, illustrations and videos on daily basis. Fotolia was the first platform which offers buyers to choose crowdsourced or professional images.Their contributors are paid the best rates on the market. That's why top artists, photographers and image-makers around the world bring their work to Fotolia. iStock only pays 15% of the royalties made from your images and Fotolia between 20% and 25% of the sale price. For every content sold via our Pay-As-You-Go system, you can receive between 20% and 63% of the sale price. I think that this is the reason why Fotolia become the leader in the European Microstock industry. There are no additional fees for registration or portfolio management and you could make thousands of dollars per month.

Everyone can use Fotolia, from professional designer and small business owner to students. There just few requirements you neet to fill:

- Be at least 18 years of age.
- Be the exclusive author of every file you present.
- An own authorization for all the rights to the elements showed in your files (e.g. property , people, products, etc.).
- Your account must have been confirmed.

So if you have a talent for photography and want to make money from it, try to sell your creations online whit help of Fotolia that offers your photos to millions of image buyers all around the world. **Registration is free and procedure is very simple:**

1. Go to Fotolia.com. and click on "Sign Up" button in the top right corner.
2. Fill the apliccation form with basic detail about you, read general terms of use and privacy policy and hit the green "Sign Up" button.
3. Confirme your email address (click on the link included in the confirmation email).

Tip: Start with Shutterstock, iStockphoto and Fotolia. With the list of those three agencies, you will be busy uploading your photos. That is the best way for to become the better artist because they all has its own standards when it comes to images you upload. Differences are in the standards of images they like and accept and which might sell well. If you learn (read master) to create pics that are accepted at all three of them, you have really made a big step to making decent money. If you do that, your photos will certainly find at least one place where customers can find and see them. And for the end, you need bother too much about the rejections. Just accept and learning from them.

Resume

There are many ways of making money online for people from all around the world. Everyone have some talents, interests which can use to make money online, they just need to know where to find them.

Opportunities are all around us. **Ways of earning money online really exist**! In this e-book, we talked about 21 awesome ways to make money online which are legitimate, well-paid options for everyone. The only thing you need to do is to think creatively about which way you can adapt skills you already have for them. If you have a computer with an Internet connection (high-speed) and your skills. Apply the knowledge that you have gained by reading this e-book and we are sure that you will make serious money online!

See you at the top!

This is our fourth e-book about making money online.

You can have a look in previous ones and learn even more about what you need to do to become successful online businessman or business women.

How to Monetize Your Niche Site with Affiiate Marketing-Beginners Guide

How to Monetize Your Niche Site with Affiiate Marketing-Advanced Guide

How to Monetize Your Niche Site with Affiiate Marketing-Expert Level

Author

Vindimear D Heart is an author, community and brand manager, blogger. He's/ her work is focused on regularly contributing to the Internet Marketing blogs and websites as well as serving as an internal SEO resource for the team. Vindimear D Heart has been involved in various high-profile roles in the SEO industry for more than seven years. He's/ her background includes working as a website writer and being a regular columnist at some of best-known Internet Marketing online publications.

Vindimear D Heart search and social experience ranges from content creation and social media marketing to SEO reporting and consulting. Vindimear D Heart's expertise in Internet Marketing tools also helps in internal tool development and testing process.

www.ingramcontent.com/pod-product-compliance
Lightning Source LLC
Chambersburg PA
CBHW080644180526
45168CB00008B/3304

* 9 7 8 1 5 1 6 8 3 9 7 8 0 *